# dress it

# dress it

## New Ideas for Delicious Dressings, Sauces, and Marinades

## RUNNING PRESS
PHILADELPHIA · LONDON

A QUINTET BOOK

© 1999 by Quintet Publishing Limited

First published in the United States of America in 1999
by Running Press Book Publishers

Printed in China by Leefung-Asco Printers Ltd.

9 8 7 6 5 4 3 2 1

Digit on the right indicates the number of this printing

ISBN 0-7624-0504-X

Library of Congress
Cataloging-in-Publication Number 98-67646

This book was designed and produced by
**Quintet Publishing Limited**
6 Blundell Street
London N7 9BH

Creative Director: Rebecca Martin
Design: Deep Creative, London
Project Editor: Debbie Foy
Editor: Deborah Gray

Typeset in Great Britain by
Central Southern Typesetters, Eastbourne

This book may be ordered by mail from the publisher.
Please include $2.50 for postage and handling.
*But try your bookstore first!*

Running Press Book Publishers
125 South Twenty-second Street
Philadelphia, Pennsylvania 19103-4399

Material in this book has previously appeared in Quintet titles.

---

### Publisher's Note

| | |
|---|---|
| **Because of the slight risk of salmonella, raw eggs should not be served to the very young, the ill or the elderly, or to pregnant women.** | **Keep garlic and oil preparations refrigerated at all times and use within 12 hours. Do not store.** |

# contents

# introduction

Dressing-up is in vogue, and nowhere is that more evident than in culinary matters. Not long ago a knob of butter on a bowl of carrots or a little mayonnaise with salad was thought of as adequate. Not any more. Classic dressings such as Italian and Blue Cheese have retained their popularity but they have been joined by a host of new and amazing dressings influenced by the world's cuisines. There are spicy cilantro and chile dressings of Mexican origin, a whole range of dressings using the flavors of the Mediterranean, peppercorn dressings from the Szechuan region of China, dressings made with peanuts from Indonesia, as well as sweet dressings based on exotic fruits such as mangoes and limes.

It isn't just salads that are dressed to impress. Dressings can be used over a wide range of other foods such as broiled or roasted fish, poultry, meat, and vegetables. Be adventurous in your combinations. Try Mustard Yogurt dressing over steamed baby potatoes, Roast Tomato and Garlic vinaigrette over halibut steaks, or Walnut dressing over wilted spinach.

Marinating is another technique that has been reinvented. No longer thought of as a fancy way of preparing meat for Chinese-style cookery, marinating has made the big time. Today, ingredients as varied as Pernod, marmalade, yogurt, and fruits are all used in delicious combinations with fresh herbs and spices.

A marinade can be wet, or a paste, or a dry rub. Place the meat, poultry, or fish in a glass or plastic bowl and add the marinade, taking care to coat all surfaces with the mixture. Generally it is best to leave the ingredients in the marinade for at least two hours—the longer the food is left to marinate the more flavor it will absorb and the greater the tenderizing effect. Slashing the food will also speed up the process. If possible, stir the food at least once while marinating. A note of caution—avoid using salt in marinades as this will draw out the juices and toughen the meat.

Because of the risk of botulism when storing homemade infused oils, always freshly prepare your dressings, keep them refrigerated, and discard any that is unused after 12 hours. Do not store infused oils, particularly those made with garlic and onion.

**Dress it** is full of easy-to-prepare dressings and marinades which will spice up your cooking in an instant. You'll be thrilled at the difference an excellent dressing can bring to the food at your table.

# relish it

## classic salad dressings

# classic mayonnaise

## Ingredients

**MAKES 1¹/₂ CUPS**

**2 EGG YOLKS** (SEE NOTE, P.4)

**2 TBSP WHITE WINE VINEGAR OR LEMON JUICE**

**1 TSP DIJON MUSTARD**

**1¹/₄ CUPS OIL**

**SALT AND FRESHLY GROUND BLACK PEPPER**

The keys to success when making mayonnaise are having all the ingredients at room temperature and adding the oil very slowly, especially at first, and whisking all the time.

Whether you use all olive oil, half olive oil and half a bland oil such as sunflower oil, or all of a bland oil, is a matter of taste. For extra character use a proportion of a nut oil. The choice of wine vinegar or lemon juice is also a question of individual taste and how you plan to use the mayonnaise.

Put egg yolks into a bowl and stir in half of the vinegar or lemon juice, and the mustard.

Add oil, drop by drop, whisking constantly. After about half of the oil has been incorporated, the rest can be added slightly more quickly, but continue to whisk until all the oil has been emulsified and sauce is thick and shiny.

Beat in remaining vinegar or lemon juice and season to taste. Add more mustard, if required.

# roast garlic mayonnaise

**Ingredients**

| | |
|---|---|
| MAKES ABOUT 1½ CUPS | 2 EGG YOLKS (SEE NOTE, P.4) |
| 2 GARLIC CLOVES, PEELED | 2-3 TSP LEMON JUICE |
| 2 SPRIGS OF THYME OR ROSEMARY | 1¼ CUPS VIRGIN OLIVE OIL |
| 2 TBSP OLIVE OIL | SALT AND FRESHLY GROUND BLACK PEPPER |

Preheat oven to 350°F. Put each garlic clove on a piece of waxed paper. Add a thyme or rosemary sprig and trickle over 1 tablespoon of olive oil. Fold up waxed paper to enclose garlic and seal edges together firmly. Put on a cookie sheet and bake for 35 to 40 minutes until garlic is soft.

Allow garlic to cool slightly then squeeze garlic cloves from their skins, into a bowl. Add egg yolks and 1 teaspoon of lemon juice. Beat hard.

Beat in virgin olive oil, a drop at a time, until half of the oil has been added. Add another teaspoon of lemon juice then slowly trickle in remaining oil, beating hard, constantly.

Season and add more lemon juice, if necessary.

# tuna mayonnaise

## Ingredients

**MAKES ABOUT 1¹/₂ CUPS**

**1** GARLIC CLOVE

¹/₂ CUP CANNED TUNA, DRAINED

ABOUT **2** TBSP LEMON JUICE

A SPRIG OF PARSLEY

**1** EGG OR **2** EGG YOLKS

(SEE NOTE, P.4)

**1**¹/₂ TSP DIJON MUSTARD

**1** CUP OLIVE OIL

¹/₂ CUP SUNFLOWER OIL

SALT AND FRESHLY GROUND
BLACK PEPPER

Tuna mayonnaise is the classic sauce to spoon over the Italian poached
veal dish, *Vitello Tonnato*, but has many other uses. For extra zest and
depth of flavor, add some chopped capers and anchovy fillets. Tarragon
vinegar can be used instead of lemon juice.

Put garlic, tuna, lemon juice, parsley, egg, and mustard into a blender.
Mix together briefly to make a smooth paste. With the motor running,
slowly pour in olive oil then sunflower oil until well emulsified and thick.

Season to taste and add more lemon juice, if required.

# aïoli

## Ingredients

**MAKES ABOUT 1¹/₂ CUPS**

**6–12 GARLIC CLOVES**

**SALT AND FRESHLY GROUND BLACK PEPPER**

**2 EGG YOLKS** (SEE NOTE, P.4)

**¹/₂–1 TSP DIJON MUSTARD (OPTIONAL)**

**ABOUT 1¹/₄ CUPS OLIVE OIL**

**1¹/₂ TBSP LEMON JUICE OR WHITE WINE VINEGAR, OR A COMBINATION OF BOTH**

Aïoli is a type of mayonnaise which has puréed garlic cloves as a base. It comes from Provence in France, where it is also sometimes known as *beurre de Provence*.

Put garlic and a dash of salt into a bowl and crush them together until reduced to a paste. Work in egg yolks and mustard, if using.

Add oil, a few drops at a time, while stirring slowly, evenly, and constantly. After half of the oil has been incorporated, add half of the lemon juice or vinegar. Remaining oil can now be added a little more quickly but sauce must be stirred in same way.

Add remaining lemon juice or vinegar, and season.

# ginger and
# green onion mayonnaise

## Ingredients

**MAKES ABOUT 1¼ CUPS**

**2 EGG YOLKS** (SEE NOTE, P.4)

½–1 TSP GINGER JUICE

½ CUP OLIVE OIL

½ CUP PEANUT OIL

**2 TBSP SCALLIONS, CHOPPED**

**FRESHLY GROUND
BLACK PEPPER**

To make the ginger juice needed for this recipe, crush a piece of peeled ginger in a garlic press. Use to dress chicken, pork, fish or shellfish, and vegetable salads.

Put egg yolks, salt, and ½ teaspoon of ginger juice into a blender. Mix briefly. With motor running, slowly trickle in the oils; add scallions almost at the end so they become finely chopped but are not reduced to a pulp.

Season with black pepper. Add more ginger juice, if necessary.

# classic french dressing

## Ingredients

**MAKES ABOUT** $1/3$ **CUP**

**3-4** TBSP OIL

**1** TBSP WHITE WINE VINEGAR

$1/2$ TSP DIJON MUSTARD
(OPTIONAL)

SALT AND FRESHLY
GROUND BLACK PEPPER

French dressing is a simple combination of oil, vinegar, and seasoning, whisked together until the oil and vinegar have emulsified. Mustard, usually Dijon, is an optional flavoring, usually in the proportion of $1/2$ teaspoon to 3 to 4 parts oil and 1 part vinegar, but it will also help an emulsion to form.

Put all the ingredients into a bowl and whisk together thoroughly until emulsified and thickened.

# coleslaw dressing

## Ingredients

**MAKES ABOUT 1¹/₃ CUPS**

**¹/₂ CUP SOUR CREAM**

**¹/₂ CUP MAYONNAISE,
BOTTLED OR HOMEMADE**

**5 TBSP CIDER VINEGAR**

**1 TSP MUSTARD POWDER**

**2 TSP CARAWAY SEEDS**

**DASH OF SUPERFINE SUGAR**

**SALT AND FRESHLY GROUND
BLACK PEPPER**

Caraway seeds, a classic complement to cabbage, give this creamy dressing a touch of distinction.

Put sour cream, mayonnaise, vinegar, mustard powder, and caraway seeds in a bowl. Whisk together until evenly combined. Add dash of sugar and seasoning to taste.

# thousand island dressing

## Ingredients

**MAKES ABOUT 1¹/₂ CUPS**

**1 CUP MAYONNAISE,**
**BOTTLED OR HOMEMADE**

**2 TBSP STUFFED OLIVES,**
**CHOPPED FINELY**

**1 TBSP GREEN BELL PEPPER,**
**CHOPPED FINELY**

**1 TBSP ONION OR CHIVES,**
**CHOPPED FINELY**

**1 TBSP FRESH**
**PARSLEY, CHOPPED**

**1 HARD-COOKED EGG,**
**CHOPPED FINELY**

**FEW DROPS OF TABASCO SAUCE**

**SALT AND FRESHLY**
**GROUND BLACK PEPPER**

The islands to which the title refers are in the St Lawrence Seaway on the Canadian border. The original 19th-century dressing did not contain mayonnaise but was simply a vinaigrette dressing flavored and colored pink by paprika pepper or tomato paste. Serve with crisp green salads, egg, potato, or shrimp salads.

Put mayonnaise into a bowl. Stir in remaining ingredients.

# caesar salad dressing

## Ingredients

**MAKES ABOUT 1 CUP**

**3** GARLIC CLOVES

**2** EGG YOLKS
(SEE NOTE, P.4)

**1** TSP WORCESTERSHIRE SAUCE

**1** TBSP LEMON JUICE

**1/3** CUP VIRGIN OLIVE OIL

**1/2** CUP FRESHLY GRATED
PARMESAN CHEESE

SALT AND FRESHLY
GROUND BLACK PEPPER

Caesar salad was invented in Tijuana, Mexico by Caesar Cardini. During the Prohibition era, Americans flooded over the border to his restaurant in search of hard liquor which they were unable to get at home. The salad was later popularized in the New York restaurant Chasens, and is now available across the nation. Needless to say, there are quite a number of versions of the dressing.

Mash garlic with a dash of salt in a bowl using a pestle and mortar. Whisk in egg yolks, Worcestershire sauce, and lemon juice.

Slowly pour in the oil, whisking constantly until well emulsified. Stir in cheese, then season to taste.

# green goddess dressing

## Ingredients

**MAKES ABOUT 2 CUPS**

**1 CUP MAYONNAISE, BOTTLED OR HOMEMADE**

**1/2 CUP SOUR CREAM**

**1 GARLIC CLOVE, CHOPPED FINELY**

**3 ANCHOVY FILLETS, CHOPPED FINELY**

**4 TBSP FRESH PARSLEY, CHOPPED FINELY**

**4 TBSP CHIVES, CHOPPED FINELY**

**1 TBSP LEMON JUICE**

**1 TBSP TARRAGON VINEGAR**

**SALT AND FRESHLY GROUND BLACK PEPPER**

This dressing was invented at the Palace Hotel in San Francisco (the hotel was destroyed in the earthquake and fire of 1906.) Although it is now usual to include sour cream in the dressing, it did not feature in the original recipe. Use the dressing for fish, shellfish, or vegetable salads.

Put all ingredients into a bowl and stir together.

# russian dressing

### Ingredients

**MAKES ABOUT 2 CUPS**

**1¹/₂ CUPS MAYONNAISE,**
**BOTTLED OR HOMEMADE**

**4 TBSP TOMATO SAUCE**

**4 TBSP DILL PICKLES,**
**CHOPPED**

**1 SHALLOT, CHOPPED FINELY**

**1 TSP FRESH**
**HORSERADISH, GRATED**

**FEW DROPS OF TABASCO SAUCE**

The original Russian dressing recipe contained caviar but serve this one with green salads, vegetables, eggs, shellfish, or cold meats.

Put mayonnaise into a bowl. Stir in remaining ingredients.

# blue cheese dressing

## Ingredients

**MAKES ABOUT 1½ CUPS**

**3 OZ BLUE CHEESE, CRUMBLED**

**1 GARLIC CLOVE,
FINELY CRUSHED**

**1 CUP SOUR CREAM
OR RICH YOGURT**

**ABOUT 1 TBSP WHITE
WINE VINEGAR**

**ABOUT 2 TBSP FRESH PARSLEY,
CHOPPED, OR 1 TBSP CHIVES,
CHOPPED (OPTIONAL)**

**FRESHLY GROUND
BLACK PEPPER**

This dressing is light, yet has a creamy taste and texture. Roquefort is a traditional cheese to use, and Stilton and Gorgonzola make a good dressing, but Danish Blue is too harsh. Blue cheese dressing is used on and with many foods, from salad leaves to baked potatoes.

Mash cheese and garlic with a fork. Mix in sour cream or yogurt, vinegar, and parsley or chives, if using. Season with black pepper.

Cover and set aside in a cool place, but not the refrigerator if possible, for several hours. Stir before serving.

# sauce vierge (tomato and olive oil dressing)

## Ingredients

**MAKES ABOUT 1½ CUPS**

**4 WELL-FLAVORED TOMATOES,
PEELED AND SEEDED**

**2 SMALL GARLIC CLOVES,
PEELED (SEE NOTE, P.4)**

**SCANT 1 CUP VIRGIN OLIVE OIL**

**2 TBSP FRESH BASIL OR
CHERVIL, CHOPPED**

**2 TBSP PARSLEY, CHOPPED**

**1 TBSP TARRAGON OR
THYME, CHOPPED**

**8 CORIANDER SEEDS,
ROASTED AND CRUSHED**

**SALT AND FRESHLY GROUND
BLACK PEPPER**

For this dressing use well-flavored, sun-ripened tomatoes and good quality olive oil. The dressing goes well with all types of salads and can also be served with broiled fish, cold chicken, or turkey.

Cut tomatoes into ¼-inch dice and put into a bowl. Stir in remaining ingredients and mix well.

Put the bowl over a saucepan of hot water, cover and leave for 30 minutes. Remove from pan and leave until cold.

# remoulade sauce

## Ingredients

**MAKES ABOUT 2 CUPS**

1½ CUPS MAYONNAISE,
BOTTLED OR HOMEMADE

2 TSP DIJON MUSTARD

3 TBSP PICKLES, CHOPPED

3 TBSP CAPERS, CHOPPED

3 TBSP FRESH PARSLEY, CHOPPED

1 TBSP FRESH
TARRAGON, CHOPPED

4 ANCHOVY FILLETS, CHOPPED

This robustly-flavored recipe adds life to cold meats, eggs, fish, and boiled vegetables, turning them into appetizing salads. As an alternative you could mix in celeriac, mustard, and lemon juice to make a more unusual celeriac remoulade.

Put mayonnaise into a bowl. Stir in remaining ingredients.

# sauce louise

## Ingredients

**MAKES ABOUT 1¾ CUPS**

1 CUP MAYONNAISE, BOTTLED
OR HOMEMADE

¼ CUP HEAVY CREAM

2 TBSP LEMON JUICE

1 TSP WORCESTERSHIRE SAUCE

4 TBSP SCALLIONS, CHOPPED

4 TBSP GREEN BELL
PEPPER, CHOPPED

FEW DROPS OF TABASCO SAUCE

A zesty sauce, particularly good with stuffed artichokes, shrimp, and crab.

Put mayonnaise into a bowl. Stir in cream and lemon juice, then add remaining ingredients.

# spice it

## herbs & spices

# parsley and lemon dressing

## Ingredients

**MAKES ABOUT ³/₄ CUP**

²/₃ **CUP VIRGIN OLIVE OIL**

2 **TBSP LEMON JUICE**

1 **TSP GRATED LEMON RIND**

2 **GARLIC CLOVES,**
**CHOPPED FINELY**

2 **TSP PARSLEY, CHOPPED**

1 **TSP SHERRY VINEGAR**

1¹/₂ **TBSP FRESHLY GRATED**
**PARMESAN CHEESE**

**SALT AND FRESHLY GROUND**
**BLACK PEPPER**

Make this dressing a few hours
ahead and leave in a cool place,
preferably not the refrigerator.
Mix again, before using in salads
with crisp lettuce leaves, such as
Romaine, and croûtons.

Mix all the ingredients together
until well emulsified.

# oregano and anchovy dressing

## Ingredients

**MAKES SCANT 1 CUP**

**3 OZ CANNED ANCHOVY FILLETS**

**A LITTLE MILK**

**1 SMALL GARLIC CLOVE, CHOPPED FINELY**

**1½ TBSP FRESH OREGANO, CHOPPED FINELY**

**JUICE OF 1 LEMON**

**⅓ CUP VIRGIN OLIVE OIL**

**1 TSP SUN-DRIED TOMATOES IN OIL, CHOPPED FINELY**

**FRESHLY GROUND BLACK PEPPER**

Use this dressing for broiled eggplants, peppers, zucchini, and onions, with tomato or green salads, or with broiled fish.

Soak anchovy fillets in milk for 5 minutes, then drain. Put them into a mortar with garlic and herbs and crush together with a pestle to make a smooth paste, slowly working in half of the lemon juice.

Beat in the oil, a drop at a time, until half has been added. Stir in remaining lemon juice then slowly trickle in remaining oil, beating constantly. Lightly stir in chopped sun-dried tomatoes and season with freshly ground black pepper.

# mint and tomato vinaigrette

## Ingredients

This dressing is good over salad leaves, with avocado or zucchini salads, or served with warm fish such as tuna, salmon, red mullet or fresh mackerel.

Put all the ingredients, except tomatoes and mint, into a bowl and whisk together until well emulsified.

Peel, seed, and chop the tomatoes, and stir with the mint into the dressing. Season to taste.

**MAKES ABOUT 1 CUP**

SCANT 1/2 CUP OLIVE OIL

1 TSP WHITE WINE VINEGAR

1 1/2 TSP LIME JUICE

1 GARLIC CLOVE, FINELY CHOPPED

1 SHALLOT, FINELY CHOPPED

3 WELL-FLAVORED TOMATOES

1 TBSP FRESH MINT, CHOPPED

SALT AND FRESHLY GROUND BLACK PEPPER

# herb vinaigrette

## Ingredients

**MAKES ABOUT 1/2 CUP**

2 TBSP WHITE WINE VINEGAR OR LEMON JUICE

SALT AND FRESHLY GROUND BLACK PEPPER

1 TSP DIJON MUSTARD (OPTIONAL)

1/3 CUP OLIVE OIL

2 TBSP FRESH HERBS, CHOPPED

A single herb or several can be used, but try to choose herbs that are complementary to the salad ingredients. Do not add them until shortly before it is to be served, otherwise they may darken.

Put vinegar or lemon juice, seasoning, and mustard into a bowl. Slowly pour in the oil in a thin, steady stream, whisking until vinaigrette has emulsified and thickened. Taste for seasoning and level of herbs, and adjust if necessary.

# tomato and basil dressing

## Ingredients

**MAKES ABOUT 1¼ CUPS**

**1 TBSP OLIVE OIL**

**2 TBSP WALNUT OIL**

**2 TBSP WHITE WINE VINEGAR**

**1 TBSP SHERRY VINEGAR**

**3 WELL-FLAVORED TOMATOES**

**18-20 BASIL LEAVES,
CHOPPED**

**DASH OF SUPERFINE SUGAR
(OPTIONAL)**

**SALT AND FRESHLY GROUND
BLACK PEPPER**

A light, fresh-tasting dressing for fish and shellfish, pasta, egg, chicken, or avocado salads. The walnut oil enhances the flavor of the tomatoes and if you are able to use well-flavored, sun-ripened tomatoes they should be sweet enough for the dressing. If not, add a little sugar.

Pour oils and vinegars into a bowl. Whisk together.

Peel, seed, and finely chop tomatoes then stir into dressing with the basil. Add a little sugar if necessary, then season to taste.

# pesto vinaigrette

## Ingredients

**MAKES GENEROUS 1 CUP**

**5-6 TBSP WHITE WINE VINEGAR**

**4 TSP PESTO SAUCE**

**2/3 CUP OLIVE OIL**

**SALT AND FRESHLY
GROUND BLACK PEPPER**

The addition of pesto sauce quickly makes a tasty, versatile dressing that goes well with green salads, pasta, and nearly all vegetable salads. Also egg, shellfish, chicken, turkey, and beef salads.

Put 5 tablespoons of vinegar and the pesto sauce into a bowl. Slowly pour in the oil, whisking until emulsified.

Season to taste and add more white wine vinegar, if required.

# herb, lemon, and caper dressing

## Ingredients

**MAKES ABOUT 1¼ CUPS**

**½ GARLIC CLOVE**

**SALT AND FRESHLY GROUND
BLACK PEPPER**

**4 TBSP LEMON JUICE**

**4 TBSP CAPERS**

**2 TBSP CHIVES, CHOPPED**

**2 TBSP DILL, CHOPPED**

**2/3 CUP OLIVE OIL**

Put garlic and a dash of salt into a mortar. Crush together with a pestle until reduced to a paste.

Stir in lemon juice, capers, and herbs. Slowly trickle in the oil, whisking until well emulsified. Season with black pepper.

This dressing goes well with shellfish, cucumber, zucchini, or egg salads, or with broiled fish, especially salmon or firm fish such as angler fish, fresh cod, and fish cakes.

# chive and
## lemon vinaigrette

## Ingredients

**MAKES ABOUT ³/₄ CUP**

**1 GARLIC CLOVE**

**SALT AND FRESHLY GROUND BLACK PEPPER**

**4 TBSP LEMON JUICE**

**RIND OF 1 LEMON, GRATED**

**1¹/₂ TSP WHOLEGRAIN MUSTARD**

**¹/₄ CUP VIRGIN OLIVE OIL**

**2 TBSP CHIVES, CHOPPED**

Use this dressing to make a light potato salad by tossing it with warm new potatoes, and finely chopped scallions.

Put garlic and a dash of salt into a bowl. Crush together, then stir in lemon rind and juice, and the mustard until smooth.

Slowly pour in the oil, whisking constantly, until well emulsified.

Add chives and season with freshly ground black pepper.

# herb, garlic, and mustard dressing

## Ingredients

**MAKES ABOUT 1 CUP**

**1-2 GARLIC CLOVES**

**SALT AND FRESHLY GROUND BLACK PEPPER**

**LEAVES FROM 4-5 SPRIGS OF THYME**

**LEAVES AND FINE STEMS FROM A SMALL BUNCH OF CHERVIL**

**1 TSP DIJON MUSTARD**

**¼ CUP RED WINE VINEGAR**

**¾ CUP OLIVE OIL**

A strongly flavored dressing, best used for more robust salads such as Niçoise salad.

Put garlic, a dash of salt, and herbs into a bowl. Crush together then stir in mustard and vinegar until smooth.

Slowly pour in oil, whisking constantly, until well emulsified. Season with black pepper.

# basil and parmesan dressing

## Ingredients

Use for salads, such as warm pasta, shellfish, green, potato, zucchini, egg, cheese, and broiled vegetables.

Put garlic, basil leaves, dash of salt, and vinegar into a small blender. Mix briefly then, with motor running, slowly pour in the oil until well emulsified.

Transfer to bowl. Stir in cheese and season with black pepper.

**MAKES ABOUT ³/₄ CUP**

**2** GARLIC CLOVES

**1** LARGE BUNCH OF BASIL

SALT AND FRESHLY GROUND BLACK PEPPER

**1** TBSP WHITE WINE VINEGAR

**¹/₃** CUP VIRGIN OLIVE OIL

**2** TBSP FRESHLY GRATED PARMESAN CHEESE

# cilantro, caper, and lime dressing

## Ingredients

**MAKES ABOUT 1 CUP**

**1** GARLIC CLOVE, CHOPPED FINELY

**1¹/₂** TSP WHOLEGRAIN MUSTARD

FINELY GRATED RIND AND JUICE OF **2** LIMES

**1** TBSP WHITE WINE VINEGAR

**¹/₄** CUP VIRGIN OLIVE OIL

**3-4** TBSP CAPERS

**3** TBSP FRESH CILANTRO, CHOPPED

FRESHLY GROUND BLACK PEPPER

Try tossing this piquant dressing with warm potatoes or celeriac, use for seafood salads, or spoon over fried foods such as fish or sliced cheeses such as feta.

Put garlic, mustard, lime rind, juice, and vinegar into a bowl and mix together. Slowly pour in the oil, whisking constantly, until well emulsified. Stir in capers and cilantro. Season with black pepper.

# salad leaves with chipotle chile dressing

## Ingredients

**MAKES ABOUT 1½ CUPS**

**DRESSING**

6 DRIED CHIPOTLE CHILES

1 SMALL ONION, SLICED

2 GARLIC CLOVES, CRUSHED

3 TBSP MEDIUM-DRY WHITE WINE

3 TBSP WHITE WINE VINEGAR

2 TBSP TOMATO PASTE

¼ PT WATER

**SALAD**

4 OZ ARUGULA

SEVERAL FRISÉE AND RADICCHIO LEAVES

1 SMALL LITTLE GEM LETTUCE

2 HEADS RED CHICORY

4 OZ BABY SPINACH LEAVES

1 SMALL RED ONION, SLICED THINLY

3 TBSP ASSORTED FRESH HERBS, SUCH AS CILANTRO, FLAT-LEAF PARSLEY, OREGANO, AND MARJORAM

Chipotle chiles give a delicious smoky flavor to the dressing. Substitute any other dried chile if preferred, or use fresno chiles for a fresher flavor.

Refresh dried chiles as follows: First, lightly roast in a non-stick pan for a few minutes, being careful not to burn or scorch the chile. Cover with very hot (not boiling) water and leave at least 10 minutes, until soft. Drain and split chiles and discard seeds. Put into a pan with remaining dressing ingredients over a gentle heat and cook, covered, for 45 minutes, or until chiles are soft and liquid is reduced by half.

Blend to a smooth purée in a blender or food processor, then pass through a sieve to remove any seeds. Reserve.

Lightly rinse salad leaves, chicory, and herbs and pat dry with paper towels. Tear the leaves if large, then toss together in a large salad bowl.

Divide chicory into single leaves and add to salad with the onion and herbs. Mix together lightly. Just before serving, drizzle with dressing and toss lightly.

# chile and cilantro
## vinaigrette

## Ingredients

**MAKES ABOUT 1 CUP**

**3 FRESH GREEN CHILES,
SEEDED AND CHOPPED FINELY**

**1/2 TSP GROUND CUMIN**

**2 TBSP CIDER VINEGAR**

**SALT**

**1/2 CUP PEANUT OIL**

**SMALL BUNCH OF
CILANTRO, CHOPPED**

Containing chiles, ground cumin, and fresh cilantro, this dressing is excellent over Mexican-style bean and corn salads.

Put chiles, cumin, vinegar, and salt into a bowl. Whisk together. Slowly pour in oil, whisking constantly, until dressing is well emulsified. Stir in cilantro just before serving.

# indonesian peanut dressing

## Ingredients

MAKES ABOUT 2 CUPS

2 TBSP PEANUT OIL

1 ONION, CHOPPED FINELY

1 GARLIC CLOVE, CHOPPED FINELY

DASH OF CRUSHED RED CHILES

1 CUP UNSALTED ROASTED PEANUTS

3/4 CUP COCONUT MILK

1 1/2 TSP SOY SAUCE

JUICE OF HALF A LIME

1 TSP RAW BROWN SUGAR

SALT AND FRESHLY GROUND BLACK PEPPER

An essential part of the Indonesian mixed vegetable salad, *gado gado*, although it is served separately rather than over the salad itself. It is also served as a dressing for warm potato, green bean, cauliflower, zucchini, or celery salads. If prepared in advance, the dressing may separate: in this case heat gently and stir in a single tablespoon of water.

Heat oil in a skillet, and fry onion until lightly browned. Add garlic and chiles and fry until the onion is golden.

Meanwhile, put peanuts into a blender and grind to a coarse paste. Stir coconut milk, soy sauce, lime juice, sugar, and nut paste, mixing well until smooth and creamy. Season to taste.

# coconut and peanut dressing

## Ingredients

MAKES ABOUT ³/₄ CUP

1¹/₂ TBSP PEANUT OIL

2 GARLIC CLOVES,
FINELY CHOPPED

¹/₄ CUP THICK COCONUT MILK

4 TSP SOY SAUCE

2 TBSP RICE WINE VINEGAR

3 TBSP PEANUT BUTTER

DASH OF RAW BROWN SUGAR

DASH OF GROUND, ROASTED,
SZECHUAN PEPPERCORNS

FRESHLY GROUND
BLACK PEPPER

Roast the Szechuan peppercorns, then grind them in a spice grinder or crush very finely with a mortar and pestle. Serve over chinese noodle or raw vegetable salads.

Heat oil in a small heavy skillet, add garlic and fry gently for 1 to 2 minutes. Add coconut milk and stir gently. Stir in remaining ingredients until thoroughly mixed.

# ginger and cilantro vinaigrette

## Ingredients

MAKES ABOUT 1 CUP

¹/₂-INCH PIECE OF FRESH
GINGER, GRATED

1 SHALLOT, CHOPPED FINELY

JUICE OF 1 LIME

1 TBSP SOY SAUCE

2 TBSP RICE WINE VINEGAR

¹/₂ CUP OLIVE OIL

1 TBSP DARK SESAME OIL

SALT AND FRESHLY GROUND
BLACK PEPPER

¹/₂ BUNCH OF CILANTRO,
CHOPPED COARSELY

Toss with salad leaves such as chicory, Romaine, watercress, or young spinach. Use for cheese salads, or to dress fish such as sea bass, tuna, or salmon, or for chicken or pork. A garnish of toasted sesame seeds complements the dressing.

Put ginger, shallot, lime juice, soy sauce, and vinegar into a bowl and whisk together.

Trickle in the olive oil, whisking vigorously, then whisk in the sesame oil. Season to taste. Add cilantro just before serving.

# saté dressing

### Ingredients

**MAKES ABOUT 2¼ CUPS**

**¾ CUP ROASTED UNSALTED PEANUTS**

**1 GARLIC CLOVE**

**2 TBSP RED CURRY PASTE**

**1¾ CUPS COCONUT MILK**

**2 TBSP RAW BROWN SUGAR**

**SQUEEZE OF LIME JUICE**

**DASH OF HOT CHILI POWDER**

Serve saté dressing over pork, beef, chicken, shellfish, or kabobs. Garnish with lime wedges.

Put peanuts, garlic, curry paste, and a little of the coconut milk into a blender and mix to a paste. Add remaining coconut milk and sugar. Mix until smooth.

Pour ingredients into a saucepan and add lemon juice. Boil for 2 minutes then simmer gently for 10 minutes, stirring occasionally to prevent sticking. Add a little water if sauce becomes too thick. Add chili powder to taste. Serve warm.

# black bean, ginger, and watercress dressing

## Ingredients

**MAKES ²/₃ CUP**

**1 TBSP SALTED BLACK BEANS, CHOPPED COARSELY**

**1 TBSP GROUNDNUT OR GRAPESEED OIL**

**2 TSP SESAME OIL**

**2 TSP FRESH GINGER, GRATED**

**2 TBSP RICE WINE**

**1¹/₂ OZ FINE STEMS AND LEAVES OF WATERCRESS**

**FRESHLY GROUND BLACK PEPPER**

Serve with fish salads of salmon or firm white fish such as angler fish, chicken, young spinach leaves, warm Chinese egg, or cellophane noodles.

Steep black beans in 2 tablespoons hot water for 15 minutes. Drain and dry on paper towels.

Put black beans, oils, ginger, and rice wine into a bowl and whisk together until emulsified. Stir in the watercress and season with black pepper.

# szechuan peppercorn dressing

## Ingredients

**MAKES ABOUT 1³/₄ CUPS**

**1 TBSP SZECHUAN PEPPERCORNS**

**3 GARLIC CLOVES**

**JUICE OF 6 LIMES**

**1 TBSP FRESH CILANTRO**

**1 TBSP FRESH PARSLEY**

**1 TBSP FRESH DILL**

**1 TBSP SUGAR**

**SALT AND FRESHLY GROUND BLACK PEPPER**

This dressing, which has quite a pronounced flavor, will lose its color if kept for more than a few hours. Serve it over duck, chicken, and cold pasta salads.

Put peppercorns into a dry small, heavy skillet and heat until fragrant. Tip into a blender and add remaining ingredients. Mix until smooth.

# toss it

fruit, seeds, & nuts

# lemon and lime cream dressing

## Ingredients

Lighter than mayonnaise, this clean-tasting dressing can be used as an alternative to dress shrimp, scallop, and lobster salads, or chicken or turkey salads.

Put lime and lemon rinds and juices, scallions, salt, and sugar into a bowl. Slowly trickle in the oil, whisking until well emulsified.

Gradually whisk in the cream. Add Tabasco sauce and freshly ground black pepper to taste.

**MAKES ABOUT 1¹/₂ CUPS**

**FINELY GRATED RIND AND JUICE OF 1 LARGE LIME**

**FINELY GRATED RIND AND JUICE OF ¹/₂ LEMON**

**4 PLUMP SCALLIONS, CHOPPED FINELY**

**SALT AND FRESHLY GROUND BLACK PEPPER**

**2 TSP SUPERFINE SUGAR**

**¹/₃ CUP OLIVE OIL**

**²/₃ CUP HEAVY CREAM**

**FEW DROPS OF TABASCO SAUCE**

# orange vinaigrette

## Ingredients

**MAKES ABOUT 1 CUP**

**4 TBSP ORANGE JUICE**

**1 TSP ORANGE RIND, GRATED FINELY**

**1 TBSP WHITE WINE VINEGAR**

**1 TSP BALSAMIC VINEGAR**

**1 SHALLOT, FINELY CHOPPED**

**¹/₃ CUP VIRGIN OLIVE OIL**

**SALT AND FRESHLY GROUND BLACK PEPPER**

Use this dressing to top a refreshing salad of thinly sliced fennel and oranges, or a grated carrot salad. With a dash of caraway seeds added, it can be used for beet salads.

Put orange juice and rind, vinegars, and shallot into a bowl. Slowly pour in the oil, whisking until well emulsified. Season to taste.

# coconut and
# lemon dressing

## Ingredients

**MAKES ABOUT 1 CUP**

**1 TBSP PEANUT OIL**

**6 OZ CREAMED COCONUT,
CHOPPED**

**2 TBSP RICE WINE**

**3-INCH PIECE OF LEMON GRASS,
CRUSHED AND SLICED THINLY**

**LARGE DASH OF 5-SPICE POWDER**

**SALT AND FRESHLY GROUND
BLACK PEPPER**

Serve with fish or shellfish, or
Chinese noodle salads. Garnish
with basil leaves.

Heat oil in a heavy skillet. Add
coconut cream and heat gently,
stirring, until it has melted. Stir in
remaining ingredients and mix well
until evenly blended.

# cal-ital sun-dried tomato dressing

## Ingredients

**MAKES ABOUT 1 1/2 CUPS**

**12 SUN-DRIED TOMATOES, SOAKED IN WATER UNTIL PLUMP, THEN DRAINED**

**2 GARLIC CLOVES**

**1 TSP DRIED OREGANO**

**1 TBSP TOMATO PASTE**

**1/3 CUP BALSAMIC VINEGAR**

**SALT AND FRESHLY GROUND BLACK PEPPER**

**1/2 CUP OLIVE OIL**

This naturally sweet dressing is excellent when served on strong-flavored salad leaves, such as arugula, or on pasta, bruschetta, or small pizza rounds. Use a high-quality brand of extra virgin olive oil for the finest flavor.

Place tomatoes, garlic, oregano, tomato paste, and vinegar in a food processor or blender, and purée.

Add salt and pepper to taste. With machine running, gradually add oil in a steady stream until well combined. Serve immediately, and discard unused dressing.

# poppy seed vinaigrette

## Ingredients

**MAKES ABOUT 1 CUP**

**1/2 TSP ENGLISH MUSTARD POWDER**

**1/4 TSP GROUND GINGER**

**1/2 RED ONION, GRATED**

**3 TBSP RED WINE VINEGAR**

**1 TBSP CLEAR HONEY**

**1 TBSP POPPY SEEDS**

**2/3 CUP PEANUT OIL**

**SALT AND FRESHLY GROUND BLACK PEPPER**

Use with avocado salads, green leaf salads such as chicory, and savory fruit salads.

Put mustard powder, ground ginger, onion, vinegar, honey, and poppy seeds into a bowl. Whisk together.

Slowly pour in the oil, whisking constantly, until dressing is well emulsified. Season to taste.

# mediterranean dressing

## Ingredients

**MAKES ABOUT 1 CUP**

**2 SUN-DRIED TOMATOES**

**1 SMALL GARLIC CLOVE**

**1 TBSP CAPERS**

**ABOUT 8 PITTED BLACK OLIVES**

**1¹/₂ TBSP RED OR
WHITE WINE VINEGAR**

**¹/₂ CUP VIRGIN OLIVE OIL**

**DASH OF SUGAR (OPTIONAL)**

**FRESHLY GROUND
BLACK PEPPER**

This dressing is ideal for a salad made of cubed firm white bread (flavored with herbs or garlic) and crisp salad leaves. It is also good spooned over broiled cheese, or tossed with pasta.

Finely chop tomatoes, garlic, capers, and olives. Put into a bowl and add vinegar.

Slowly pour in the oil, whisking constantly, until well emulsified. Season with sugar, if using, and black pepper.

# walnut dressing

## Ingredients

**MAKES ABOUT 1/2 CUP**

1/4 CUP WALNUT HALVES

3 TBSP OLIVE OIL

3 TBSP WALNUT OIL

2 TBSP BALSAMIC VINEGAR

SALT AND FRESHLY GROUND
BLACK PEPPER

Walnut dressing has an affinity with
cheese, watercress, and spinach
salads, and goes well with cabbage
and firm salad leaves.

Preheat oven to 350°F. Spread the
nuts on a cookie sheet and bake, about
15 minutes, until crisp and browned.
Chop the nuts. Put oils and vinegar
into a bowl. Whisk until well blended.
Add nuts and season to taste.

# mango vinaigrette

## Ingredients

**MAKES ABOUT 1¼ CUPS**

**1 RIPE MANGO,**
**PEELED AND SLICED**

**1 SMALL TO MEDIUM**
**FRESH RED CHILE,**
**SEEDED AND CHOPPED**

**1 TBSP WHITE WINE VINEGAR**

**½ CUP OLIVE OIL**

**SALT AND FRESHLY**
**GROUND BLACK PEPPER**

Use to accompany smoked chicken, turkey, or pork.

Put ingredients into a blender and mix until smooth.

# roast tomato and garlic vinaigrette

### Ingredients

**MAKES ABOUT ³/₄ CUP**

**1 LARGE TOMATO**

**3 PLUMP GARLIC CLOVES, PEELED**

**1 TSP SHERRY VINEGAR**

**¹/₄ CUP VIRGIN OLIVE OIL**

**SALT AND FRESHLY GROUND BLACK PEPPER**

Use over broiled red bell peppers, zucchini, eggplant, and onions, or toss with warm pasta.

Preheat broiler. Broil tomato and garlic until softened, charred, and blistered. Let cool then peel them. Seed and chop the tomato.

Put garlic and tomato into a blender and mix until smooth. Add vinegar then, with motor running, slowly pour in the oil until well emulsified. Season well and serve.

# creamy orange and hazelnut dressing

## Ingredients

MAKES ABOUT ³/₄ CUP

3 TBSP ORANGE JUICE

2 TBSP SHERRY VINEGAR

2 TBSP HEAVY CREAM

1 TBSP ORANGE LIQUEUR
(OPTIONAL)

SCANT ¹/₂ CUP HAZELNUT OIL

¹/₂ CUP HAZELNUTS,
TOASTED AND CHOPPED

SALT AND FRESHLY GROUND
BLACK PEPPER

This dressing works well over salads of broiled salmon with lamb's lettuce, spinach, and watercress. It also complements beet, carrot, fennel, and chicory.

Put orange juice, vinegar, heavy cream, and liqueur into a bowl. Mix together. Slowly pour in the oil, whisking, until dressing emulsifies. Add hazelnuts and season to taste.

# sweet and savory dressing

## Ingredients

MAKES ABOUT 1 CUP

2 TBSP CLEAR HONEY

5 TBSP PORT

JUICE OF 3 LEMONS

SALT AND FRESHLY GROUND
BLACK PEPPER

Use for fruit salads served as a first course, such as mixed melons. Chopped mint, grated fresh ginger, or a sprinkling of ground cinnamon are good finishing touches.

Put honey, port, and lemon juice into a bowl. Stir together thoroughly, then season to taste.

# whisk it

## yogurt, cheese, & cream

# mustard yogurt dressing

## Ingredients

**MAKES ABOUT 1 CUP**

**1 CUP PLAIN YOGURT**

**1 TBSP SCALLION,
CHOPPED FINELY**

**1 TBSP DIJON MUSTARD**

**1 TBSP PARSLEY OR
CHIVES, CHOPPED**

**SALT AND FRESHLY GROUND
BLACK PEPPER**

A light but well-flavored dressing for spinach, potato, or a range of other vegetable salads.

Put all ingredients into a bowl and stir until evenly mixed. Cover and chill before using.

# warm minted lemon cream dressing

## Ingredients

**MAKES ABOUT ¾ CUP**

**4 TBSP SOUR CREAM**

**JUICE AND RIND OF ½ LEMON, GRATED FINELY**

**1 TBSP FRESH MINT, CHOPPED FINELY**

**5 TBSP PLAIN YOGURT**

**SALT AND FRESHLY GROUND BLACK PEPPER**

This is ideal for young, sweet peas, sugar snap peas, baby carrots, and baby corn.

Put sour cream into a small saucepan and heat gently. Stir in lemon rind and juice, and mint. When warmed through, stir in the yogurt, taking care not to let dressing overheat. Season to taste.

# yogurt and tahini dressing

## Ingredients

Popular throughout the Middle East, yogurt and tahini dressing is served with egg salads, coleslaw salads, with warm new potatoes, or crudités.

Whisk lemon juice into the yogurt. Add garlic. Slowly stir in the oil until well mixed.

Beat in tahini then add ground cumin and seasoning to taste. Cover and chill. Use within 12 hours.

**MAKES ABOUT 1 CUP**

**3-4 TSP LEMON JUICE**

**6 TBSP PLAIN YOGURT**

**1-2 GARLIC CLOVES, CHOPPED FINELY**

**1/3 CUP OLIVE OIL**

**4 TBSP TAHINI PASTE**

**DASH OF GROUND CUMIN**

**SALT AND FRESHLY GROUND BLACK PEPPER**

# herb cream cheese dressing

## Ingredients

**MAKES SCANT 1 CUP**

**1/2 CUP FULL FAT SOFT CHEESE**

**2/3 CUP BUTTERMILK**

**1-2 TSP LEMON JUICE**

**4 TBSP FRESH MIXED HERBS, CHOPPED OR 2 TBSP FRESH TARRAGON OR BASIL, CHOPPED**

**SALT AND FRESHLY GROUND BLACK PEPPER.**

Mixing buttermilk with soft cheese makes a dressing that is creamy but not too rich. The fresh flavors of the herbs also give it a light taste. Use it for cooked vegetable salads or salads containing chicken.

Put soft cheese into a bowl. Slowly pour in the buttermilk, stirring, until evenly blended. Add lemon juice. Mix in the herbs. Season to taste. Serve chilled.

# yogurt and
## orange dressing

## Ingredients

**MAKES ABOUT 1 CUP**

**3 TBSP ORANGE JUICE**

**1 TBSP CLEAR HONEY**

**1 CUP PLAIN YOGURT**

**SALT AND FRESHLY GROUND
WHITE PEPPER**

Use for first course fruit salads, such as melon and orange, and garnish with fresh mint.

Stir orange juice into the honey. Add orange juice mixture to the yogurt and stir together. Season to taste. Cover and chill in refrigerator.

# lemon yogurt vinaigrette

## Ingredients

**MAKES ABOUT 1½ CUPS**

**6 TBSP PLAIN YOGURT**

**2 TBSP SHERRY VINEGAR**

**¼ CUP OLIVE OIL**

**2 TSP DIJON MUSTARD**

**JUICE OF 1 LEMON**

**ABOUT 2 TBSP WATER (OPTIONAL)**

**DASH OF SUPERFINE SUGAR**

**SALT AND FRESHLY GROUND BLACK PEPPER**

This is a lighter tasting, fresher alternative to ordinary vinaigrette, and can be used in the same ways. Walnut or hazelnut oil can be substituted for half of the olive oil, depending on the salad.

Put yogurt, vinegar, oil, and mustard and lemon juice into a bowl and mix together. If vinaigrette is too thick add a little water. Add sugar and seasoning to taste.

# light herb sauce

## Ingredients

**MAKES ABOUT ¾ CUP**

**⅔ CUP SOUR CREAM OR PLAIN YOGURT**

**2 TBSP FRESH HERBS, CHOPPED**

**1 TSP SHALLOT, CHOPPED FINELY**

**SALT AND FRESHLY GROUND BLACK PEPPER**

A simple, quick sauce that can be flavored with any herb. If you prefer a milder dressing, leave out the shallot. Serve the dressing over green salads, warm, new potato salads, vegetable salads, or warm, white beans such as cannellini.

Put sour cream or yogurt, herbs, and shallot into a bowl. Stir together and season to taste.

# ricotta and
## blue cheese dressing

### Ingredients

**MAKES ABOUT 2 CUPS**

**5 OZ RICOTTA CHEESE**

**5 OZ STILTON OR OTHER BLUE CHEESE SUCH AS GORGONZOLA OR ROQUEFORT**

**5 OZ SOUR CREAM OR PLAIN YOGURT**

**SALT AND FRESHLY GROUND BLACK PEPPER**

A piquant cheese is best for this dressing to contrast with creamy ricotta. Flavor it with garlic, scallions, or herbs such as parsley, rosemary, or sage. Use for warm pasta, potato, rice, lima or cannellini beans, lentil salads, or over crisp lettuce leaves.

Crumble ricotta and blue cheese into a bowl and mash lightly together with a fork. Slowly pour in sour cream, mixing well with a fork until dressing is smooth. Season with a little salt and plenty of black pepper.

# oil-free cream vinaigrette

**Ingredients**

Chill the dressing well and pour it over crisp green leaves, or mix with cold cooked vegetables. Do not make the dressing too far in advance or the vinegar will thicken the cream.

Put garlic into a bowl, add a dash of salt and crush together to a paste

Separate egg white from yolk; reserve egg white for garnishing salad. Add egg yolk, mustard, and vinegar to the bowl and mix with garlic. Stir in the cream and add sugar and pepper to taste. Cover and chill.

**MAKES ABOUT 1¼ CUPS**

¹/₂ GARLIC CLOVE

SALT AND FRESHLY
GROUND BLACK PEPPER

1 HARD-COOKED EGG

¹/₂ TSP DIJON MUSTARD

2 TSP TARRAGON VINEGAR

1 CUP LIGHT CREAM

DASH OF FINE
GRANULATED SUGAR

# horseradish and sour cream dressing

**Ingredients**

**MAKES ABOUT 1 CUP**

³/₄ CUP SOUR CREAM

4 TBSP FRESH OR BOTTLED
HORSERADISH, GRATED

2 TSP LEMON JUICE OR
WHITE WINE VINEGAR

SALT AND FRESHLY GROUND
BLACK PEPPER

Spoon over sliced tomatoes, toss with boiled cauliflower for an inspired salad, or serve with sliced cold beef.

Pour sour cream into a bowl. Stir in the horseradish and lemon juice or white wine vinegar to taste. Season to taste. Cover and chill.

# sweeten it

## sweet dressings & marinades

# strawberry wine marinade

## Ingredients

**MAKES ABOUT 1¼ CUPS**

**4 TBSP SUGAR**

**2½ CUPS DRY WHITE WINE**

**4 LARGE RIPE STRAWBERRIES**

A simple but sophisticated marinade, just right for making an impressive light dessert of pears, plums, peaches, apricots, cherries, lychees, or mangosteens.

Put sugar and wine in a wide, shallow saucepan and heat gently, stirring until sugar has dissolved. Boil gently, without stirring, for 3 to 4 minutes.

Add strawberries to the pan and simmer for 6 to 7 minutes until reduced by half, and syrupy. Pour over prepared fruit and let cool. Chill before serving.

# white wine marinade

**MAKES ABOUT 1½ CUPS**

**1¼ CUPS DRY WHITE WINE**

**¼ CUP SUGAR**

**LONG STRIP OF
LEMON OR LIME RIND**

**6 LEMON BALM LEAVES**

**DASH OF GROUND MACE**

A light, summery marinade that combines well with oranges, melons, peaches, and pineapples. Pour it over the fruit while it is hot and leave the fruit to steep until cold.

Pour wine into saucepan. Add sugar, lemon or lime rind, lemon balm leaves, and mace and heat gently, stirring until sugar has dissolved. Bring to a boil and bubble for 1 minute.

# cardamom butter dressing

**Ingredients**

**MAKES ABOUT 1 CUP**

**½ CUP UNSALTED
BUTTER, DICED**

**SEEDS FROM 6 CARDAMOM
PODS, CRUSHED**

**2 TBSP LIME OR ORANGE JUICE**

**2 TBSP WHISKY OR BRANDY**

**2 TBSP CONFECTIONERS'
SUGAR**

This fragrant, buttery dressing spiked with whisky or brandy adds an air of luxury to fruit kabobs or broiled fruits. The best fruits for this treatment are tropical fruits such as pineapples, mangoes, papayas, bananas, or pears. For a variation, use 2½ tablespoons finely chopped fresh ginger in place of cardamom.

Melt butter in a small saucepan over a low heat. Stir in remaining ingredients until evenly blended.

# red wine marinade

## Ingredients

**MAKES ABOUT 1½ CUPS**

**1¼ CUPS DRY RED WINE**

**⅓ CUP RAW BROWN SUGAR**

**LONG STRIP OF ORANGE RIND**

**1 TSP GROUND PUMPKIN PIE SPICE**

**¼ TSP NUTMEG, FRESHLY GRATED**

**2-INCH PIECE CINNAMON**

**5 CLOVES**

Pour the hot marinade over sliced ripe pears, halved, ripe plums, strawberries, or halved, ripe peaches. If the fruit is not ripe enough to eat as it is, gently stew it in marinade until tender, before steeping.

Pour wine into a saucepan. Add sugar, orange rind, and spices and heat gently, stirring until sugar has dissolved. Bring to a boil and bubble gently for 1 minute.

# sweet ginger, cinnamon, and rice wine marinade

## Ingredients

**MAKES ABOUT ⅔ CUP MARINADE; ABOUT ¼ CUP DRESSING**

**½ CUP RICE WINE**

**2 TBSP FRESH GINGER, GRATED**

**1 TBSP CANDIED GINGER, CHOPPED FINELY**

**½ CINNAMON STICK**

**DASH OF SUGAR**

Use as a marinade and a dressing for broiled fruits—first steep the fruit in it, then remove the fruit and broil it. Boil the dressing that is left until syrupy, and brush over the hot fruit. Decorate the fruit with extra chopped candied ginger and serve with lime or lemon wedges.

Put ingredients into a small saucepan and bring just to boiling point. Pour over the fruit and let cool. Using a slotted spoon, scoop out fruit. Strain marinade into a small saucepan and boil until syrupy.

Broil fruit until lightly browned then pour over the ginger and rice wine syrup.

# orange, lemon, and honey dressing

## Ingredients

**MAKES ABOUT ³/4 CUP**

**¹/2 CUP ORANGE JUICE**

**2 TBSP LEMON JUICE**

**ABOUT 2 TBSP CLEAR HONEY, OR TO TASTE**

A simple, light summer dessert is made by pouring this dressing over melon balls (a combination of different melons is best). Orange or grapefruit slices, peaches, nectarines, or strawberries work well too.

Pour orange and lemon juices into a bowl. Add honey and stir until melted.

# ginger dressing

## Ingredients

**MAKES ABOUT 1¹/₂ CUPS**

¹/₄ **CUP SUPERFINE SUGAR**

²/₃ **CUP WATER**

²/₃ **CUP GINGER WINE**

**2 PIECES STEM GINGER PRESERVED IN SYRUP, CHOPPED FINELY**

**JUICE AND RIND OF 1¹/₂ LIMES, GRATED FINELY**

Tropical fruit salads containing lychees, mangoes, pineapple or papaya, oranges, clementines and tangerines, grapefruits, and pears marry well with this dressing.

Put sugar and water into a saucepan and heat gently, stirring, until sugar has dissolved. Bring to a boil then simmer for 1 minute without stirring. Remove pan from heat and add ginger wine, chopped stem ginger, and lime rind and juice.

Pour over the prepared fruit and let cool. Chill before serving.

# spiced citrus syrup

**Ingredients**

**MAKES ABOUT 2 CUPS**

**1¹/₄ CUPS WATER**

**¹/₂ CUP SUPERFINE SUGAR**

**2 LARGE STRIPS
OF LIME OR LEMON RIND**

**2 LARGE STRIPS
OF ORANGE RIND**

**¹/₂ TSP GROUND GINGER**

**1 CINNAMON STICK**

**LIME OR LEMON
JUICE, TO TASTE**

Use for pouring over fruit salads, particularly with tropical fruits such as mangoes and papayas, melons, oranges, pears, and grapes.

Pour water into saucepan, add sugar and heat gently, stirring until sugar has dissolved. Add fruit rinds, ginger, and cinnamon and bring slowly to a boil. Remove from heat, cover and leave until cold. Chill.

Before using, strain syrup and add lime or lemon juice to taste.

# leave it

marinades & spice rubs

# herb marinade

## Ingredients

**MAKES ABOUT ²/₃ CUP**

**¼ CUP OLIVE OIL**

**2 TBSP LEMON OR LIME JUICE OR WHITE WINE VINEGAR**

**1 GARLIC CLOVE, CHOPPED FINELY**

**4 TBSP FRESH HERBS, CHOPPED**

**FRESHLY GROUND BLACK PEPPER**

A versatile marinade that can be used for meat, poultry, fish, or vegetables. Be sure to use a good, well-flavored olive oil. The herbs can be varied according to the food to be marinated and what is available.

Mix ingredients together. Chill and serve.

# orange and herb marinade

## Ingredients

**MAKES ABOUT 1¼ CUPS**

**JUICE OF 2 ORANGES**

**²/₃ CUP DRY WHITE WINE**

**3 TBSP OLIVE OIL**

**1 TSP FRESH MARJORAM, CHOPPED**

**1 TSP FRESH THYME, CHOPPED**

**1 TSP FRESH ROSEMARY, CHOPPED**

**1 GARLIC CLOVE, FINELY CHOPPED**

**FRESH GROUND BLACK PEPPER**

White wine adds a special flavor to this marinade. Use it for pork, chicken, game, duck, and lamb.

Put ingredients into a bowl and whisk together until well blended.

# yogurt and
## chile marinade

### Ingredients

**MAKES ABOUT ³/₄ CUP**

¹/₂ CUP PLAIN YOGURT

1 ONION, CHOPPED FINELY

2 GARLIC CLOVES

2 FRESH RED CHILES,
SEEDED AND CHOPPED

JUICE OF 1 LIME

CHILI POWDER (OPTIONAL)

SALT AND FRESHLY GROUND
BLACK PEPPER

Use this marinade to spread over
shelled large shrimp before broiling,
or for chicken kabobs.

Put yogurt, onion, garlic, chiles, and
lime juice in a blender. Mix ingredients
to a paste. Add chili powder if using,
and season to taste.

# spiced yogurt marinade

## Ingredients

**MAKES ABOUT 3/4 CUP**

2/3 CUP PLAIN YOGURT

2 GARLIC CLOVES

1 TBSP FRESH
GINGER, CHOPPED

1 TBSP GROUND CUMIN

2 TSP PAPRIKA PEPPER

1/2 TSP GROUND CHILI

1/2 TSP GROUND CARDAMOM

A popular marinade to use for chicken drumsticks and thighs to be broiled or barbecued. It can also be used for fish or lamb.

Put ingredients into a blender and mix together until smooth.

# mandarin marinade

## Ingredients

**MAKES ABOUT 1 CUP**

**2 TBSP MANDARIN
OR ORANGE MARMALADE**

**1 TSP FRESH GINGER, GRATED**

**1 GARLIC CLOVE,
CHOPPED FINELY**

**1/4 CUP WHITE WINE VINEGAR**

**1/4 CUP ORANGE JUICE**

**1/4 CUP LEMON JUICE**

**1/2 CUP OLIVE OIL**

**FRESHLY GROUND BLACK PEPPER**

A slightly sweet, yet sharp, citrus-flavored marinade spiked with fresh ginger that is good with beef, lamb, pork, wild and reared duck, and pigeon.

Put all ingredients except oil and seasoning in a saucepan and heat, stirring, until marmalade has melted. Simmer until reduced to 1 cup. Pour into a bowl and let cool.

Stir in oil and season with black pepper to taste.

# dried apricot marinade

## Ingredients

**MAKES ABOUT 1 CUP**

²/₃ CUP DRIED APRICOTS,
SOAKED OVERNIGHT

2 TBSP OLIVE OIL

1 LARGE ONION, SLICED

1 GARLIC CLOVE,
CHOPPED FINELY

1¹/₂ TSP CURRY POWDER

1¹/₂ TBSP WHITE WINE VINEGAR

1¹/₂ TBSP LEMON JUICE

DASH OF CAYENNE PEPPER

1¹/₂ TSP SUGAR

FRESHLY GROUND
BLACK PEPPER

Curry powder adds a spicy note to the deep fruit flavor of dried apricots to make a marinade that transforms lamb, chicken, pork, or duck.

Put apricots into a small saucepan and add enough of their soaking liquid to just cover. Bring to a boil then simmer gently for 15 to 20 minutes or until tender.

Let cool slightly, tip into a blender and mix to a purée.

Heat oil in a skillet, add onion and garlic and fry until softened and golden. Stir in the curry powder for 1 minute then add apricot purée and remaining ingredients. Stir well. Bring to a boil then let cool.

# coconut marinade

## Ingredients

**MAKES ABOUT 1 CUP**

²/₃ CUP BOILING WATER

**3 OZ CREAMED COCONUT**

**1 TSP LIME JUICE**

**1 SHALLOT, CHOPPED FINELY**

**1 GARLIC CLOVE,**
FINELY CHOPPED

**1 LEMON GRASS STALK,**
CRUSHED

**SEEDS FROM 3 CARDAMOM**
PODS, CRUSHED

¹/₂-INCH PIECE FRESH
GINGER, GRATED

¹/₂ TSP GROUND CUMIN

**FRESHLY GROUND**
**BLACK PEPPER**

This Eastern-style marinade works well with firm fish such as angler fish, or with chicken, turkey, pork, or lamb.

Pour boiling water over coconut and stir until smooth. Add remaining ingredients and cool.

# saffron and
# lemon marinade

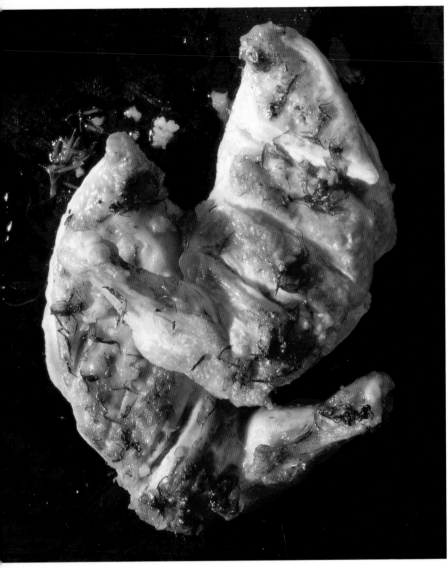

## Ingredients

**MAKES ABOUT ³/₄ CUP**

**DASH OF SAFFRON THREADS**

**1 TBSP HOT WATER**

**2 GARLIC CLOVES,**
**CHOPPED FINELY**

**JUICE OF 1¹/₂ LEMONS**

**2 TBSP WHITE WINE VINEGAR**

**GENEROUS ¹/₂ CUP**
**MILD OLIVE OIL**

**FRESHLY GROUND**
**BLACK PEPPER**

Saffron and lemon combine to make
an elegant marinade that originated in
Italy. It is used for zucchini and jumbo
shrimp, but is also good with scallops,
firm white fish, or chicken breasts.
Two tablespoons of chopped capers
can be added for piquancy.

Put saffron in a bowl, pour over the
water and let steep for 5 minutes. Add
remaining ingredients. Whisk together.

# thai-style marinade

## Ingredients

**MAKES ABOUT ³/₄ CUP**

**2 GARLIC CLOVES, CHOPPED FINELY**

**1 FRESH GREEN CHILE, SEEDED AND CHOPPED FINELY**

**2 TBSP FRESH CILANTRO, CHOPPED**

**2 TBSP FRESH BASIL, CHOPPED**

**2 TBSP FRESH MINT, CHOPPED**

**¹/₂-INCH PIECE FRESH GINGER, GRATED**

**¹/₄ CUP LIME JUICE**

**1 TBSP FISH SAUCE**

**1 TBSP SESAME OIL**

**FRESHLY GROUND BLACK PEPPER**

Typical ingredients of Thai cooking produce a well-flavored marinade that suits broiled tuna, salmon, or swordfish steaks, firm white fish such as angler fish and cod, and chicken.

Put ingredients into a bowl. Stir together until well mixed.

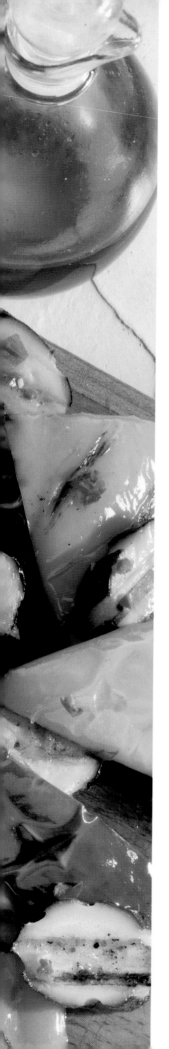

# marinade for broiled vegetables

**Ingredients**

**MAKES ABOUT ³/₄ CUP**

**¹/₂ CUP OLIVE OIL**

**1 TBSP SHERRY VINEGAR**

**1 GARLIC CLOVE, CHOPPED FINELY**

**1 SHALLOT, CHOPPED FINELY**

**1 FRESH RED CHILE, SEEDED AND CHOPPED FINELY**

**SALT AND FRESHLY GROUND BLACK PEPPER**

Steep the broiled vegetables in this marinade, overnight at room temperature, then serve as an antipasto accompanied by good, firm bread to mop up the juices.

Put ingredients into a bowl and mix together.

# tandoori marinade

## Ingredients

**MAKES ABOUT 2 CUPS**

**1** ONION, CHOPPED COARSELY

**4** LARGE GARLIC CLOVES

**1** OZ FRESH GINGER

**4** TBSP LEMON JUICE

**1** CUP PLAIN YOGURT

**1/4** CUP SUNFLOWER OIL

**1** TBSP GROUND TURMERIC

**1** TBSP GROUND CORIANDER

**1** TSP GROUND CUMIN

**1/2** TSP GROUND CINNAMON

**1/2** TSP GRATED NUTMEG

**1/2** TSP FRESHLY GROUND
BLACK PEPPER

**1/4** TSP GROUND CLOVES

**1/4** TSP CHILI POWDER
OR CAYENNE PEPPER

An authentic-tasting Indian tandoori marinade for skinned chicken portions, cubes of lamb, raw jumbo shrimp, or firm-fleshed fish.

Put onion, garlic, and ginger into a blender and process until chopped. Add remaining ingredients and mix until smooth.

# white wine marinade

## Ingredients

**MAKES ABOUT 1¼ CUPS**

**2 TBSP MILD OLIVE OIL**

**1 SHALLOT, CHOPPED FINELY**

**1 CARROT, CHOPPED FINELY**

**2 JUNIPER BERRIES, CRUSHED**

**2 BLACK PEPPERCORNS, CRUSHED**

**1 SPRIG OF CELERY LEAVES, CHOPPED**

**2 PARSLEY STEMS**

**1 BAY LEAF, TORN**

**1 SPRIG OF THYME**

**1 SLICE OF LEMON**

**ABOUT 1¼ CUPS DRY WHITE WINE**

Lighter than a red wine marinade, this recipe is good with farmed pigeon and rabbit, young partridge and pheasant, lamb, and chicken, turkey, and pork.

Put ingredients into a bowl and stir. If meat is not covered by the marinade, add more wine.

# lime and pernod marinade

## Ingredients

Lime marries well with the anise flavor of Pernod to make a marinade that is ideal for seafood, especially raw shrimp and scallops, and cuts of fresh haddock.

Put ingredients into a bowl and mix together thoroughly.

**MAKES ABOUT 1 CUP**

**4** TBSP PERNOD

JUICE OF **2** LIMES

**1** SMALL GARLIC CLOVE, CHOPPED FINELY (OPTIONAL)

**1** TSP FENNEL SEEDS, LIGHTLY CRUSHED

**1**$^1$/$_2$ TBSP FRESH CILANTRO, CHOPPED

$^1$/$_3$ CUP OLIVE OIL

FRESHLY GROUND BLACK PEPPER

# cilantro, lime, and vermouth marinade

## Ingredients

**MAKES ABOUT** $^3$/$_4$ **CUP**

**3** TBSP FRESH CILANTRO, CHOPPED

JUICE AND RIND OF **2** LIMES, GRATED FINELY

**2** TBSP DRY WHITE VERMOUTH

**2** GARLIC CLOVES, CHOPPED FINELY

$^1$/$_4$ CUP OLIVE OIL

TABASCO SAUCE (OPTIONAL)

FRESHLY GROUND BLACK PEPPER

Dry white vermouths are flavored with blends of herbs and spices. As each producer has its own special blend, the taste (and quality) of vermouths varies between brands. If you want to add a bit of heat, add a drop of Tabasco sauce.

Put ingredients into a bowl and mix together.

# salmoriglio

## Ingredients

**MAKES ABOUT 1¼ CUPS**

**1 GARLIC CLOVE**

**1 TBSP FRESH PARSLEY, CHOPPED FINELY**

**1½ TSP FRESH OREGANO, CHOPPED**

**ABOUT 1 TSP FRESH ROSEMARY, CHOPPED**

**¾ CUP VIRGIN OLIVE OIL, WARMED SLIGHTLY**

**3 TBSP HOT WATER**

**4 TBSP LEMON JUICE**

**SEA SALT AND FRESHLY GROUND BLACK PEPPER**

In Sicily, salmoriglio is used for fish to be broiled or barbecued. Sicilians believe that the only way to make a really good salmoriglio is to add seawater; in the absence of this ingredient use sea salt for seasoning. Salmoriglio can also be served warm as a sauce to accompany the fish.

Put garlic, herbs, and a dash of salt into a mortar or bowl and pound to a paste with a pestle and mortar.

Pour oil into a warm bowl, then, using a fork, slowly pour in hot water followed by lemon juice, whisking constantly until well emulsified. Add herb and garlic mixture, and black pepper to taste.

Put bowl over a saucepan of hot water and warm for 5 minutes, whisking occasionally. Let cool before using.

# spice rub for fish

## Ingredients

**MAKES ABOUT 9 TABLESPOONS**

**2 TSP LEMON RIND, GRATED**

**1 TSP DRIED TARRAGON, CHOPPED FINELY**

**1 TSP DRIED BASIL, CHOPPED**

**1/2 SMALL GARLIC CLOVE, CHOPPED FINELY**

**1 TBSP PAPRIKA PEPPER**

**1/2 TSP CAYENNE PEPPER**

**FRESHLY GROUND BLACK PEPPER**

Lemon, tarragon, and basil in this recipe make it particularly suitable for fish.

Put ingredients into a bowl and stir until mixed thoroughly.

# cajun spice rub

## Ingredients

**MAKES ABOUT 7 TABLESPOONS**

**1 PLUMP GARLIC CLOVE**

**1/2 SMALL ONION, CHOPPED**

**1 TSP DRIED THYME**

**1 TSP DRIED OREGANO**

**1/2 TSP GROUND CUMIN**

**1/2 TSP MUSTARD POWDER**

**1/2 TSP FRESHLY GROUND BLACK PEPPER**

Use mainly with red meats. Dried basil, sage, or fennel can be substituted for the dried thyme or oregano.

Crush garlic and onion with a mortar and pestle. Mix in remaining ingredients.

# simple spice rub

## Ingredients

**MAKES ABOUT 3 TABLESPOONS**

**1 TSP CUMIN SEEDS**

**1 TSP CORIANDER SEEDS**

**SEEDS FROM 6 CARDAMOM PODS**

**1/2 TSP BLACK PEPPERCORNS**

Use this simple spice rub for large cuts of salmon or tuna.

Heat a heavy skillet, add seeds until fragrant, shaking pan frequently.

Tip spices into a small blender, a spice grinder, mortar, or a bowl. Grind finely, or crush finely with the end of a rolling pin.

# index